Richmond Public Library
Richmond, California

CORA FRY

CORA FRY

by Rosellen Brown

W · W · Norton & Company · Inc · New York

A selection of these poems first appeared in *Ms.* Magazine, March
1977.
Two of these poems appeared in *Redbook,* December 1976.

Library of Congress Cataloging in Publication Data
Brown, Rosellen.
    Cora Fry.

    I. Title.
PS3552.R7C6   1977   811'.5'4   76–42989
ISBN 0–393–04455–6
ISBN 0–393–04461–0 pbk.

ISBN 0 393 04455 6 cloth edition
ISBN 0 393 04461 0 paper edition

1 2 3 4 5 6 7 8 9 0

for Leone Stein

who *believes* poetry

CORA FRY

I want to understand light years.
I live in Oxford, New Hampshire.
When, then, will the light get to me?

The year I die
there'll be no snow.

Look, Nan, the
first shy snow

half falling.
Like moths I

shook out once
from a coat:

they fell down
slowly, so

slowly, and
some woke up

halfway out
into the air.

The rest fell
to the floor

still folded.

Nan, do you think moths dream?

All the men
are on the plows.
It's snowing up-
side down now.

My father
runs this show.
Here he comes, slow,
riding high,
a roar, a
yellow eye
in the ice-fog.

Some men hate him
good. But his
followers
follow in his
slippery footsteps
casting salt,
snow on snow,

December
manna.

I.

"Fry," I said
when he touched me on
my breast. "Do you think
of women,
other women, when
you're touching me there?"

In the dark
I could feel him blink—
butterfly
kiss like I give Nan
on the cheek.
"Sometimes," he said, "sort
of to crank
it up." He half-shrugged
but couldn't move much.
"Don't worry,"
and put his mouth there.
"No one you know."

II.

I thought I'd
try it too. I made
a dozen
faces come bend down
to kiss me,
all neighbors and Frank
from work—but
scared, I turned my head
so hard Fry
said "Hey kid,
should I go brush my teeth
again?"   I
gave my mouth to him
and saw black.
It takes something I don't have
and don't want. So it's Fry now
forever.

I go on Sunday
for some mystery.
But Reverend Merman
takes my hand and milks
it like an udder.
I blame myself but
at the door he dries
me out until I
crack. Gossip seeps in,
face powder, after-
shave, sermon on hope,
oh Merman, mermaid,
I give a dollar
(what with inflation
that saves half a soul)
and the hymn. Jesus
himself could sit down
beside me here and
find me out to lunch:

Chicken.   Rice.   Green peas.

One bad winter
my father poached
a deer and I died

thousands of hard
separate deaths
waiting for the

sheriff to come.
The blue light swung
across my wall

one snowbound night.
I stopped breathing.
I woke up Sam.

But it was just
the deputy,
fat Lloyd the tease,

coming to get
Daddy, his plow
and all, to pull

some foreign car
out of his field.
"Some kid got throwed

clear in a bank,
but he hit hard."
I clamored till

I got to come,
in Dad's army
blanket, shivering.

The boy was still
lying in blue
shadows, his arms

out like a snow
angel. He woke
after a while,

blood in his mouth,
swearing he had
only one beer.

The sheriff laughed
and winked at us.
Lloyd muttered "Bull . . ."

Quarter to four
on a moony
night in late March

I swallowed hard
and the deer went down.

I saw Chickering Webb today.
He put his whole hand on my thigh
once in the high school library.
I kept smiling and took it off.
That was the day before he went
crazy, and holed up in a house
with Judy Carney. Poor Miss Sleigh,
it was her house they chose to have
their orgy in. They defamed all
her father's books (Frank Sleigh the judge),
they gummed the walls with Crisco and
they gashed the sheets and cracked her bed.
Nobody ever said Judy
went crazy too. She wouldn't press
charges or tell us anything.

Chip thinks people stop
when he can't see them.

The summer people
load their cars and go
out of Oxford's sight,
far out of mind—though
every December
the Johns send a card
crammed with skyscrapers
and lit store windows
to whet my envy.
This year a tiny
car dragged a huge tree
through downtown traffic.

It's a game we play,
postmark to postmark.
Fist raised against fist.
For Oxford this year,
I sent a single star.

When the snow
got up to the window frame,
grainy as
sugar, each crystal a face
in a crowd
and the crowd silent for death,

do you know,
I wanted a field pale green
with sheep-sorrel—
warm and sour,
those light clover heads shaking,
"Everything's shaggy, newborn. Lie down here
and eat me!"

What are friends for, my mother asks.
A duty undone, visit missed,
casserole unbaked for sick Jane.
Someone has just made her bitter.

Nothing. They are for nothing, friends,
I think. All they do in the end—
they *touch* you. They fill you like music.

The moonless night
the ice hill
the snow without shadows

are mine because
I need them.
I drive down the long slope

in first, waiting
to lose hold
and slip to the bottom.

They'll find the car
pulverized
and my shadow for shame.

But it all holds:
luck, gears—sand
to the stop sign.
Bless the sweet town grit!

Joe Fox
sent his kids away
to school.
I think
if they'd been some way
special—
too smart
or sick or dumb . . .
To me,

Joe said,
they're special: they're mine.
Then what
the hell
does that make mine, asked
Father.
Makes 'em
yours, I guess, said Joe.

Sam beat
the buttons off Tom's coat
for that,
and I
loved Meg so much I
stuck my
tongue out
at her for a month.
Cut her,

Cut her,
Father taunted,
see if
she bleeds
red or white or
don't you think it's
blue now?

I go to work because it pays.
I go to work to get away.
I go to work to change my face.
I go to work to wash my hands
and wear a wig to save my head.
(I leave mine home.)
I go to work to be unknown
and in the kitchen sweating rain
I put a heavy tray down full

and watch the new man watching me.
What messages between his eyes
and mine there's room for here. . . . He's thin
as someone's undernourished son.
If I go ask for some glasses,
depending on my voice and where
my shoulders are, compared to his,
I could make room on his pillow
for my head, with or without wig.
I move my tray the other way.

Felice moves then, smiling her gap-
tooth grin. Her thighs, I think, open
and close, mouth breathing mostly in,
chattering at men endlessly,
wanting to be shut, not sweetly.

Felice has stopped two babies quick.
Times she thought they were taking care.
"Don't trust them, Core, with a blind nun.
They could care less. No matter how
they watch your ass, it's yours to watch."

The salesmen's convention
means ass cooked to order,
complained about, drinks spilled,
can't I sit on their lap,
see what they've got for me,
"a very special tip."

I put tapioca
and coffee down, smiling,
smiling as if I'm deaf
until I hear this one
shark-shouldered manager
lean to his friend and say
"That Billie Holliday,
before she got big-league,
some café in Harlem,
brought change between her *lips*.
And I don't mean her mouth,
pal, I don't mean her mouth."

I slam his second cup
of coffee, not well aimed—
I'd love to singe his lap
so he'll see purple pain
next time he gets it up
for waitress, wife, or whore.
It splashes on his cuff.
I'll live without his tip.

Nan curled in my lap.
Look at the picture: spaghetti legs!
I think I was happiest right then,
when she pulled my breasts
right inside out, like party favors . . .

"That's what they're for, Nan,"
I tell her when Chip pats them gently.
When she needs to know
I'll warn her men only think they own
your breasts. When Fry bends
to them, sometimes it feels like Nanny
or Chip, and I cry.
"Did I hurt you, hon?" he'll say. I swear
they let down milk for him.

The flowers won't grow
in the north window.

Grandmother Rule
I know went mad.
She starved to bone
and broke herself.

Mother says all
the women in
the family do,
this way or that,

which leaves some room
for Nan and me.
When it comes time
to read her will

we'll pick our pain
slowly and well:
the family jewel.

The closets are going to explode.
The table is going to collapse.
The sink is sinking.
The door just slams and slams.
The baby's crying, where's his sister?
Don't jump on me, my bones are empty.
My joints are being washed and ironed.
I'm getting an extra hour of sleep.
Before there is no more to heal up,
I'm taking the cure: *I pass. I pass.*

Fry says a word
in my poor ear
I could do with-
out. In the dark
all of me frowns.
He'll be sorry
when he gets there.

Reverend Merman
tried to convince us
only the seasons
are real. They *prevail*
is how he said it.
And, friends, they *triumph*.

They do. But meanwhile—
what a bother—here
we are. Here I am.
Rain's in the bucket,
cow's in the pea patch,
the pigs want dinner
and so do the kids.

I think I'll tell them
when winter prevails
on them, they won't be
hungry anymore:

they'll be snowchildren
in the great triumph
of time over tooth
and nail. I'll tell them,
Go melt on God's fool.

I watch my cousin Valerie
who lives at the top of Brick Hill,
riding Sim's arm, smiling, smiling.
She's young, it's enough just to find
some dark place to lie down with him,
no steering wheel, no mosquitos,
and know that everybody knows.
She listens to him talk football.
She prods him and laughs a little.

Doesn't she know the end's written?
When he sees her lie in the light,
finds one hair under her nipple,
she's got her Tupperware together,
he puts his ear to her swollen
belly for the first child only.
He says she was a good listener,
he watches the ball come toward him
out of the snow of the TV,
he catches it. Now it's the ball
of his gut, tight with fries and beer.

After her third the doctor winks:
"I took that husband-stitch for you,
dear." He thinks that's what holds husbands,
the tuck he takes in the yard goods.
He's a husband, doesn't he know
they want to graze in new meadow?
What holds them is what lets them go.

The diving crew
is under ice.
My father says
muffled goodbyes,
walks to the hole
and disappears.

We stand knotted
in a corner
of the wind-wall,
away from the
mother whose child
stiffens far down
in a stone shroud.

We don't know her,
this visitor
who brought her son
for evergreens
and frozen ponds,
a white Christmas
up in Oxford.

We only hear
her voice rising
to beat against
the wind's sharp wall.

Bubbles rise. My
silver father
stands dripping ice.
Shaking he spits
the child out whole,
and then he cries.

That table:
white oblong
blue-bordered
enamel,
chipped and clean.
Hit it right
with a spoon,
it rang out
loud for you.

Our kitchen's
all in it.
'45?
'48?
The baking—
the bread pail
hitched on tight,
screwed with that
big silver
butterfly;
me cranking
our breakfast
for the week.
The turkey
set on its
buttered rear
like a dog
met with an
accident.
The berries
giving up
their hard stems.
My homework
mama cleaned
all around
with her rag.

Her house dress—

pink and green.
Bobby sox;
mother in
red loafers;
me with my
winking dimes.

Sentiment
hides under
the blue rim
out of sight
like chewed gum.
Was it mine,
that childhood?
Sweet and soft. . . .
Now see me
saving it,
even when
it gets too
hard to chew.

Did you know during
the second world war

they turned the lights out
"in the country" too,

and listened for planes
roaring in German?

Even New Hampshire
had targets, though God

only knows which hill
we thought they wanted.

I was a child called
Cora Pearl Hubberd

you could hear crying
all over town,

shamelessly. I thought
I was about to

die. Nothing fancy:
just die in the dark
of war, of missing
my father.

My cousin Norb died in a tree
by sniper fire in Anzio.
I always pictured a monkey
and in my head changed the subject,
that was so disrespectful.

All I remembered of Norbert

from Keene, smart enough for glasses,
was how he peed in the bushes
visiting us when he was twelve.
How when he pulled his zipper up
he said, "Don't look at me like that.
Sometimes a man has got no choice."

I was staring hard at his face
that was very blond and pink veined
to keep from watching how his hands
tugged and propped up and then tucked back
the intricate thing he carried
sheathed, the way my brother hid his.

Worse than the monkey, when I heard
he died I saw his silver arc
that spattered on the day lilies
saying NORBERT WAS HERE and gone.

All the places
I've never been

                    Minnesota
                    Greenwich Village
                    Daytona Beach

I don't really
want to go there

                    but just to see
                    how people look

with thousands of
grandmothers from

                    foreign countries
                    (none in English)

Would the difference
(mother says yes)
make me nervous?

My father
says choice rots
the bones like
candy rots
the teeth.

I have a neighbor
who is always deep
in a book or two.

High tides of clutter
rise in her kitchen.

Which last longer, words,
words in her bent head,
or the clean spaces

between one perfect
dusting and the next?

Up to East
Oxford, the distant cousins

of rich men
live scratching in their good names

right on the
blacktop shoulder where all the

action is.
NIGHT CRAWLERS   BODY WORK   BRAKES

DRINK FRESCA
Their trailers rust. Their old cars

stand grazing
like horses put to pasture.

Chip runs like a squirrel
his cowlick   his tail

And Nan is old
enough to smile
like a daughter-
in-arms. Secret.
No teeth showing.

They do gnaw me
sometimes.
Their voices grind
fine, my
thumbs, my liver.

I can't
be a weapon,
it would
be too easy
to pinch, to kill,
to say
some word they won't
forget.

And if I died
would they
remember me
shouting?

Fry's hands have life lines
traced black to the bone.
He rests them against
my weak-white shoulder
and I shouldn't wilt.

Fry who walks through worlds
I can barely see,
fixing things that have
no voices: Brakes.
Clocks.
They're the animals
he feeds tenderly
or gives a light shove
to ease their movement.

On the bureau now
our old healed clock glows
under its warm skin.

You can do
anything alone
anything but
laugh out loud

We watch them hoist a streetlamp
over the bridge at the creek.
The stiff crane squeaks and lunges.

Why do we need a night light?
The dark outside my bedroom
is the safest dark there is:
sweet-smelling, familiar.
Glow worms wink up from the road
after rain. The moon comes back
and it shines like melting ice.

Now I study hard shadows
that were never there before.
I wait for someone to bolt
out of the light toward my door.

Coming home late from work,
I stopped the car one long thirsty minute
on the hilltop near my father's meadow.

Something plunged and tossed in the center
like a show animal in a lit ring.

He threw his head, he shook it free of air,
his legs flung whichway. There were the antlers,
a forest of spring twigs that rose and dived,
dancing. *Singing,* for all I knew, glassed in.

I rolled my window down
knowing I'd lose him, and I did: he ducked
into nowhere. But I had that one glimpse,

didn't I, of the animal deep in
the animal? Of his freedom flaring

only a quick blink of light? I think spring
must be a crazy water animals drink.

I used to
play here but
the field was
so much bigger

I squint to understand
how they can make bombs
of themselves, and light them.

Think. Think. Your child is dead,
someone's to blame.
You watch a bottle hit

the school bus. Your house burns
on purpose. You're a doll
the whole world sticks pins in.

The ones who need vengeance
are not the avengers—
only their kid brothers.

(Our yellow bus blurs by,
stops in its wide green frame:
Nan's head bobs to its place
at the door. She's home free.)

Fry says they just do it
to terrify their mothers.

In this sun
the wood grain
of the shed
is water.
The whole wall
is water.

Pretend to
throw a stone.
Watch it sink,
rippling out
from the hollow
heartwood.

Up the road over Snow Creek
our nearest neighbors Mister
and Mrs. Thaddeus Cole
at home in the steep brick house

look down on us from so high
you'd think they lived on a cliff.

I met her on the creek bridge.
Would I clean her house, she begged,
only so nice, no nicer?

"Can you see ladies slippers
behind that rock?" I asked her.
She never moved her coiled head.
"They look like tongues, not slippers!"
Then Nan came along dirty
on her bike and Mrs. Cole
looked sick. "Good morning," she said,

and went back up the blacktop
to her peonies and her rooms
full of good help, satisfied.

Nan goes to the cemetery
with her class: with that young teacher.
Two by two they paper the old
stones, tape over the brittleness,
turn their crayolas flat side up
(peeled back to the orange and purple),
and rub until the facts take shape
under their innocent fingers.

(Wives to both sides of the CAPTAIN,
who outlived even his MOTHER.
And the little bastard called JAS.
outside the limits of the yard,
no coarser ash than his judges.)

"I've got a baby!" my Nan squeals.
Delight. "What do you think killed it?"
Horror tickles her. She bends down.
The blunt carved face is like a slate
frog, crude as though the child worked it
herself. *LYDIA ANN Returned*
How well I remember that one,
I spent such years on my scuffed knees
worshipping true love, true loss, gone,
hardened, all of it, to mossed stone.

Like a blind child, Nan feels the dates.
She twitches fingers, counting up.
Soon she'll get to the hardest part
"wonder drugs" and "hygiene" can't stop:
that Lydia Ann would be dead now
no matter what. No matter *what*.

The mailman, Drew Teague,
puts his wheels against
my petunias thick
as faces crowding
around the mailbox.
He tugs the rusty
door open and squints
inside: no red flag
means no mail to go.
Listen to me, Drew,
if I had something
to write to someone
well out of earshot
I'd put your flag up,
call to you, *Toro!*
What's happened today
that's worth a postcard?

You bring me two bills,
an ad for snow tires,
and a letter from
my brother who is
famous nowadays
for living with a
girl named Fran in sin
at a safe distance
"to hurt his mother"
where such things are done.
Oh, he's coming home.
I mean, they are.
Well. He'll turn to me,
Sam will, and, smiling,
forgive *me,* his eyes
wide to take me in.

I would have lived with
no one but my books.
The men in old books.
Even they would need
to struggle to get
a smile from me, let
alone much more. Sam

introduced me once
to someone who said
"Smile, you're on Candid
Camera!" and I did.
But he didn't; he
left the way I think
men also leave when
they have made you smile
wide everywhere. I
never lived in sin
or even mischief.

Now when I do dream
of luscious freedom
it's not to be needed.
To be just alone . . .

Muskrat. Muskrat.
Trapped at the tooth-
pick ankle, when
you pull you are
raking yourself
to the soft dark
center. You gouge
your groin with what
edges you find—
can opener,
stone-lip, blunt flint,
what's the difference,
they're all like teeth.
You saw, you chew,
forward and back,
raising a smoke-
trail, hot, quiet,
over your head.
A snarl: come free
you roll, hobble,
you start a new
life on three legs.

Big game-hunters
Chip and Craig Fry,
checking the trap,
will pick your leg up,
shake it, bloody
knotted short string
trailing a rag
of web, and curse
you. "Double cross."
(Fry to his son,
angry. Chip pouts
to please his dad.)

Fry cracks your bone,
wishbone easy
in his tight fist.
The leg sails, lands
on leaves, becomes
a crooked twig,
or an inchworm.
They turn to lunch.

In my kitchen,
blotting water
stains off the forks,
the child-safe knives,
I can see you:

By now you are
under the cliff,
under the mountain,
eating your pain.

Linda Swain, my old friend,
at the gas pump gazing—
gazing's the word—across
Route 8 to the graveyard.

Why has her long sweet hair
gone gray like my mother's?
Why haven't I seen her
for years? I look right through
the Class of '61
as though we're made of glass.

Linda was getting out
but, first mistake, she let
Tom in. She's pumping gas
for him. He lets her crawl
under a car sometimes
(hooray for women's lib)
and drain the sludgy oil
into the common pail.

From the far, the graveyard, side
I watch her with my arms
full of DUBL-STRENGTH bags
(milk, kool-aid, and cat food).
We're two small girls who aren't
allowed to cross ourselves.

We found the gravestone
of the first mistress
of a quarter of this house.

Her quarter would have been fire-
place and keeping-room.
This was the barnyard.
Sitting right here, see
my old maple hers, and young,
and this stump with its hundred
pale rings in full-shadowed blossom.

Where I sip iced tea
she spun wool and wove
with her competent daughters,
and pushed her needle.
I do complain and mope
too much, Mistress Jonah Hoyt.
I do. I turn the channel
to strangers' angers.

Because I see such others
you never heard of,
and they make me want.
Because they drag their empty
afternoons and full evenings
across my vision, I want.

Is it all the same,
life measured by love
in spoonfuls, silver
or soft Woolworth tin?
Never more hard nor easy?
What did you covet?

If you had three good chickens
you were envied a season.
Did you keep your waist?
Did you go to Boston?
Did your children live?
(Imagine the breasts

of the young mother of eight—
long and veined with blue—
mirrored in her husband's eyes
that he remembered
when he went for a soldier. . .

In the long grasses
that soaked the hem of your dress,
in Captain Hoyt's high bedstead
receiving a child
in modest silence,
did you do better
than tolerate yourself?

Carrots and peas, beans and brussels sprouts,
they all go into the ground on cue
from the feel of the air, soft evenings.
I come out right with the mourning dove,
his loony alto song; bend spotting
where the tiny bright identical
double wings poke up out of thick dirt.
Each year I doubt, each year they prosper.
I soothe their rows with tepid water,
I tend their margins, tuck and pull up,
housekeep the wildness where I may, so

when our woodchuck comes, he has his feast
neat as a salad.
                    I will not use
Fry's 22. He says I'd rather
buy my greens at the A & P and
look at my shorn rows like a mother
who's lost her children to the plague,
and cry.

Last night I had this dream:

I didn't mark the rows
and where I planted chard
and trusted it would grow
without a sign to tell
it how,

a mass of flesh,
veiny and deep, with hair
matted like something smashed,
hunched waiting in the row.

I turned it with my shoe
and it rolled to the light:
infant faces swarming
with those lip-colored worms
that say your soil is good.

I will not forgive Fry
planting that dream in me.

Chip, remember this
always—how you thought
the merry-go-round
would take you away,
the red and white horse
canter off across
the town green. How you
stood in the stirrups
calling "Goodbye! Goodbye,
Mommy!", crying
and waving, but brave,
going. Holding on.

When you saw me come
round the second time,
I got to see your face.

Slipping
between the cool sheets of the
water

I am concentrating
on the lives of squashes:

the St. Pat scallop, thick
and placid, a ruffled
pale girl in baby fat.
This slick zucchini, striped,
clever, the racing car
of squashes, the greyhound.
And here the zeppelin,
my pale blue hubbard pumped
with nothing like hot air.
Hiding among their wild
leaves turned up like human
palms, their toothed stems that bite,
they love to surprise me.

How does a family
of nine hundred cousins
survive in such cool peace,
such silence? I hold them
in my apron still warm.

I catch the tomato,
haul it out of water,
strip it down quick to soft
flesh, oozing hard gold seeds,
drop it through the fat neck
of the bottle. It spreads
haunches with its sisters,
settling in sheer bubbles,
softening in itself.

These days I could buy cans.
I can't. I love the fat
human sprawl of the fruit
slipping through my fingers,
the patient shelf keeping
till deep January;
then opening up the seal
on the best day of summer.

This is no baby skin—
Chip?
You are a new apple.
If
I take a healthy bite
I
get to the star of seeds,
right?

I'm leaving.
Say goodbye
to mother.

Gone fishing
said Mister
Man, you go

to sleep and
don't wait up.
Where is he?

Slip around,
I can see
that happens

(though not to
Fry and me.
He *never.*)

But to go
with these friends
I don't know,

new around—
beer guzzlers,
baby wives—

to Boston—
some Red Sox—
red *garters,*

maybe. And
come home dead
in the legs,

in the eyes,
smelling like
Tillie's rose.

Go away
Fry, I said.
Go lie down

overnight
with Carl Yaz,
wake up late,

roll her back,
say hello
from Cora.

Put it there, country.
When you go
leave a ten
on the bureau.

*You are not
my husband.*

I hit the tree
at thirty.
It came toward me
and I saw the bark,
long finger-scratches
down its back.

No ambulance
no scrooo-reee   go
get the road clear
for here comes   who

Tom Fox found me
his cruiser slammed
its wheels right up
I hurt the tree

not a word Tom   not
a blessed word
Poor Cora   he
whispered and my

fingers loosened
on the steering
wheel   I bit down
on blood   on his

tinfoil shield   his
tongue going *Poor
Cora   Poor Cora*

Cora Fry
I said.
I do not want to die.
I am not dead.

I only need—
What did he say?
I want to see
him cry.

My white gown
parts in back.
No one can see
my devil cleft.
No one will ever
have to touch me
anywhere
again. I'm free.

They can
put you back together
but you
see   you come in small parts.
If there's
one missing   some big one
then they send to
Boston   but they might not
have it

I wouldn't feel this way because of "sex."

"Sex" just comes and goes
like sap running up and down a maple.
And men, my mother
always knew, have no
control, out the spile the sap comes running.
Sometimes when it boils it can even be sweet.

It isn't the vow
that I thought he meant.
But doesn't he owe
me more at home, here in the hand-built bed
where he won't let me read
because of the light,
on the sheets I bleach,
in the room I dust,

than he owes those men?
But Fry's a pal,
one of the fast boys all of a sudden.
They laughed about us
going to Boston—
"a night off the old
lady"—"the dead wood!"
while our ears burned red,
me and their kid wives here for the having.

The "sex" I forgive.
It was the laughing.

Mother said "Marriage
is like driving a
car. All you can do
is worry about
yourself. You can't stay
wide-awake sober
for somebody else,
or keep him on the
right side of the road."

The neighbors listened
all unvisited
in their quiet beds.

"I make the whole bed,
mother, not my side."

She shook her head, tired.
I have brought her shame—
not that my husband
cheats but that I bruise
so easily.

Who digs her old car
up to its fenders
into an oak tree
and gets dragged out mad,
not even sorry?

"Well, you'll never know
the things I could tell."

"What can you tell me?"

My mother looks down
onto her used breasts.
Her ankles are soft,
her legs lavender.

"Women are boring,
Cora. Every month
they make the same mess.
Every wedding day

sign the same bargain.

We all lie right down
under a ton weight
and then we can't move.
And then we're surprised.
Well, what can you think
but we deserve it?"

On the next bed floats
the lacy remains
of a grand old dame
eaten like a shawl
by famished white moths.
She has their moth-voice.

The farmer's wife nods,
nods in her fat. Hair
decorates her face,
chin whiskers. All wrong,
her signals got mixed,
all wrong. She is her
husband now. He wastes,
still wanting a wife.

We are not boring,
ma. We are just drilled
with imperfections:
holes and moles and eyes

to watch, retreating,
the same backs over
and over. Maybe
the ones who leave us—
husbands, children, cats—
maybe they're the ones
who make me yawn: left
foot in front of right
plodding to freedom.

I'll bet they're even
boring to God who
sees their backs as often
as any ordinary woman.

Trundling home
from the hospital
lightheaded
gasping in the sun

(Remember
Nan fresh in my arms
sexless in
her yellow blanket
I stood on
this hospital porch
drinking light
with my own new eyes)

Widowed now
by my own fury
buried to the waist
in bad blood

the hinges of my
thighs will rust

The weekend shift.
Work keeps me clean.
All the faces
I am smiling
at are strangers.
Some smile back, some
yell like husbands.
I take a towel
and scrub my hands
clean for the health
department, clean
for my conscience
like a good girl
before dinner.
Father used to
review my nails
and then say grace.
I go out front
with a full tray,
plastic woman
cool to the touch
in the brisk wig
Fry despises.

In the cloakroom
while I'm working,
my confusion
curls in my coat
pocket like a
smooth snail, also
cool to the touch,
soft parts drawn in.
On my break I
finger it. Go
out there to touch
pity, my small stone.

The man smells some desperation.
Frank stacks the dishwasher full
to overflowing and turns
to slow me down with his eyes.

Do I wear pain like a wild slash
across my cheek? Does he know
I'm thinking of giving up
men for beer and cigarettes?

In the dry cool of the cloakroom
he makes his quaint high-school move:
hand on my wrist, hard. Eyes closed.
What damn fools they don't mind being!

I left work
in good light

but halfway
it began

to thicken
like pudding.
Smoke pudding.

I drove slow
into clouds

with the wheels
off the ground

and when I
stopped the car

was lathered
like a horse
just run home.

I was so
sad. So sad,

I wish I
knew strange words

to say it,
a mourning

language. Lost,
I drove through

a cloud bank
so heavy

it crushed ev-
erything flat,

and I haven't
come out yet.

He was smiling, leaning,
when I shrugged on my coat.
Shadow steeped in shadow,
the whites of his eyes bright.

> My eyes close against him.
> Sometimes my real life is
> enough: Dishes. Pansies.
> Grape-skin holding back flesh.
> Arc of the bridge over
> the river. Fog tonight.
> Chip's rounded brown shoulder.
> Touching his rubber thigh,
> a handful of that warmth.
> Nan's moon smoothness: all for
> my blind fingers to touch.

> *Skin is all you need, Frank.*
> What makes a breast finer
> than a baby's shoulder?
> Why would you like to hold
> my hips and not a child's,
> turning, sharp, in your palm?
> *Warmth is what we need, Frank.*
> Anyone's living breath.
> I get it where I can.
> I choose my small kingdom.

This knight in his freedom—
"Cora," he said to me
hard, through angry teeth.
"Cora, you're wrong. There is
no choice. You have two hands.
Two legs. Take both. *Take both.*"

What an old
dull story:
TEMPTING THE GOOD WIFE
(WHO HAS HER REASONS)

I let him—
in the parking lot—
put his face
up against my face.
Only his straw cheek
on my neck.

He swallowed my mouth.

Fry. I am
a virgin again,
weak with shock
to feel under his
uniform that magic
worm turn stone.

We stood locked
till it turned again.

Rain-logged.
Tear-logged.

"A good thing it's warm,
we'd have a storm like '48."

This post-
card's washed

clean. Who was it from?
Did Frank write to say "Forget it"?

Or Fry
from his

side of the bed: "Dear
wife, dear Cora, how do you do

me this
cruel way?"

Mistress
J. Hoyt

swirls the permanent
black ink to say "Shame."

Avon
Lady

threatens, "Come, come,
it's time to buy a new blusher."

It's me.
Just me—

a piece of paper
waiting like a headstone:

What will there be in the end,
the very end,
to say?

Storm high.
Power's off.

Out on the road
a candle wanders
into the dark night's mouth.

When you begin to see them
there are more dark corners than light.

I could hide in one and not be missed
until the children wake. God protect me.

I am my neighbor's candle wavering down
the long hill, flaring, till the wind
        snaps off my head.

My children nuzzle me.
They pull me back to them.
They see like everyone
I drift. I come undone.

Their father calls their names
over my head. Fishing
with Chipper, puzzling Nan,
too slippery to catch.
They ride their bikes past me
over my head.
                    He casts
his children in a ring
to battle my children.
But none of them will win—
they'll hobble, bleed, and cry,
and lose us both trying.

Now I'm drifting to sleep
stalled in the front window.
Let them go, all of them
back over my head, back
over the road's dark crest,
glide off the edge of the world
so I can sleep it off:

my long tired motherhood,
my nights as Mrs. Fry
that must have come out of a bottle—
why else the occasional singing,
and all that idiot trust,
fooling with this stranger?

My father looks away from me.

I should have married a farmer.

If I am irresponsible
behind the steering wheel again
he'll take my keys or turn me in.

(Fry ought to do it but he won't.)

What Father knows about Oxford
stays with the plows in the garage
downtown. What I know about it
should hover in my own kitchen,
over the range, maybe, like smoke.
It should not get out the window
where all of Oxford is breathing.
Next time they're loading the sander
or grading a washed-out shoulder,
it should not come back to him in
the filthy mouths of his own men.

My father looks away from me.
Now that harsh smoke floats between us.
It will not stay in my kitchen.
It will not settle out with time.
Mother waves her hands at the smoke
she knows well. My father's loving
face is gray and spoiled.

I'm sorry.

He's moved on,
the way men do.
His clean uniform
hangs on the cloakroom pole
waiting to be filled again
by someone between moves.

(Instead of leaving
the women change
their hairdos.)

I'm sorry he's gone.
I didn't get
to say yes
or no.

The Boston bus
is always late.
I count on it.

Nan flips pages,
Chip sleeps, wakes. Nan
needs the bathroom.
"It's a closet,"
my skeptic says.
I pick her up
over the gaping
hole. She holds her
breath till her feet
touch solid ground.
A careful girl.
I only wish
care made a damn
bit of difference
in the field of
set traps that wait
to snarl her feet.

Touching some shoulders
and every seat,
Nan dances down
the rocking aisle.

Fry in Boston
forgot his wife.

I am Fry's wife
in Boston.

Now I know how to survive the city:
If you have come stark naked, you can dress
yourself in the kind indifference of crowds.
If you come tired, you can sleep with strangers.
Everything is possible, nothing is
possible. Go empty and come home full,
go full and come home empty. As you like.
Word will never seep over the state line
of what atrocities you have done here.

Park Street.   I cower behind my children.

The old witch thrusts one hand, to the elbow,
in the trash basket. It rocks
and steadies. One banana
black as a stick. A bottle
of vicious green soda turned to swamp scum.

My children point. They knead my hand and stare,
impolite. Can you see her
ready herself for bedtime,
pull her toes in through their holes,
wrap her killed nose in a sock for warming?

I'll bet she thinks she's Sheba lying back
in her coal bin. No one puffs
at her door, or in her ear.
She is how used and lonely
you can get. She makes Charity hide out

panicked, behind the Prudential Center.
Did the moon ever move her?
She hung such lovely laundry . . .
What a gathering of flies
inside her open coffin.
But they find she's all seamed up.

She makes me float and wander.
Keep me warm, children, keep me warm.
Need me.

Why do we need the Public Gardens—
this is Nan—
when we live in a Private Garden
of our own?

❖

My caterpillar
Chip says, from the bench
he's hanging from:
Too many feet, mom.
Now can we go home?

❖

Mom looks at her hands.
Like her worn face, lined
with what is called "life"
by some optimists
who hunt down the deep
folds for "character."

Oh, the old joke—half-
full? Half-empty? Half
lived? Half died? Pale now
and ready to make
peace because peace is
where you can go barefoot
and empty-handed
without protection.
Anger, like Boston
(to quote my wise son)
has too many feet.
Let's go find some quiet.

In the fall dark
under no moon
the bus steals back
through closed-down towns.
Candia, Bow,
the mild hills of
sleeping Claremont.
Our driver pulls
quietly up
to the locked doors
of all the banks.
A cat burglar
would make more noise
twirling the locks
of jewel safes.
They gape like tombs
for a second
and then slam shut
without a sound.
What does he leave
in that briefcase?
Secrets, secrets,
money maybe,
maybe better:
potions, lovers'
vows, terrible
threats. What does he
take? We're his sack-
ful of sleepers
with smiles on our
faces, strangers
head to head. I
sit bolt upright
waiting for hope
to get past me,
confidently
to put its hands
inside my chest,
to slow my breathing
but let me live.

Fry takes
the sleeping babies
one by one
from me.

Tucked back
in their own blankets,
he kisses
their eyes.

I see
he walks stiffly
as though he's
been *still*. . .

And just
as well. Sat still
and worried,
swayed in the

tidal pull
that brought me home
and still could
drown us all.

I turn
to him. I reach
and just touch him.
Careful now.
I take him back.

Something
flares a second
and in its small light
I see our faces:
almost calm.

the first frost
my God   like
death you know
it's coming
but you mourn
you never
quite believed

iced leaves   limp
marigolds
smothered black
a battlefield
squash blossom
survivors
gold   grinning

this morning
I looked out
where winter
is waiting
in the field
white as a
Halloween
ghost   but real

the wheel turns faster
going down
with the year

Boots: in a box
under the bed.
I prop them like
rubber book ends.
Two clean snowsuits
hang on these pegs
till cold chases
the children quick
into their arms.
Fry takes hot lunch
in his thermos.

At five o'clock
he tracks snow paws
onto the rug.
But it's too warm—
they glow once, then
blink out like old stars.